Withering Away

Vidhi Shah is a writer and poet. A native of Hyderabad, Telangana, she is a student of St. Joseph's Public School. She hopes that her work will bring a revolution, someday.

PAPER PALACE PUBLISHING
web: *paperpalace.in*

This is a work of fiction. Names, characters, places and incidents are either the product of the author's imagination or are used fictitiously and any resemblance to any actual person, living or dead, events or locales is entirely coincidental.

ISBN: 978-81-940678-5-6
Price: Rs. 199

Withering Away

Vidhi Shah

PLAYING PRETEND

Then I get asked if I really am,
What I pretend to be,
I say this is a world of complete anonymity,
No one is what they pretend to be,
They shield their truth with a pretty face,
Filters and adjustments until nothing stays,
A stench of truth never sets us free,
Tell me then, who is that someone you would pretend to be?
The mysterious or the bold one..?
Or the cynic that never approves of fun,
The walking dilemma stinking of jealousy,
Or the one too filtered to look pretty,
How do you say you're at least a bit true
Lost in translation, How do you then find you,
Trying to be someone else
You never knew...

REVIVAL

And I found the calm after the storm again,
I found the gleam of colors after thundering rain
Things like these tend to get better, every day,
You know the beauty of shades after everything black and grey
The calamities sweep over and the sunshine is out to see,
Every thought caged, is now set free
The royal stigmas, the contradictions and monotony,
Goes on and on until
It has a deepening silence
Of its own

THE WRONG ANSWERS

And that's the last time I let you stay
Can you see us, slipping away
Into the dark embers of flame,
But can't I wish for us to stay the same?
Pretend that it's been alright again
If I could tell you I haven't said
Those stories to anyone, been so afraid,
I didn't lie, those lies were true
Secrets kept to me and you
And that was the last time I let you be
The wrong answers to my mystery.

FAR AWAY

Because some day you'll go far
Some day you'll go far away,
And I shall hope for you to stay
Right there
Because I wasn't taught to obey
Every little word, you used to say,
And that's why I hoped for you,
To go far away; Never turn to me
Unless you have to be,
That certain someone I once knew,
So then I plead and I pray for you
Go to those unknown places you always wanted to;
Those lonely days which you shall replace with someone new
And then the air will never be so tricky again,
Hope you get off that pretend pain
So I tell you to go far far away
Enough for me to not ask you to stay,
And maybe, enough for you
Just enough for you to never look at me and then away,
So I leave my door half open today

AUTUMN

You told me you loved the way,
The leaves on the trees seemed to stay
Then the autumn came in, rushing through,
The trees lost everything including you

REPLACE

I can't make you wait for me,
In a changing world, no subtlety,
In the oath of time and promises so true,
I can't make you wait, so I must replace you

I can't say that I'd be there,
Can't make any promises, intentions bare,
In the awakening night where nothing's fair
I can't say I'd be there, may you find a spare

I can't wish anything for you,
Can't say what I want, when I have to,
In the deepest of despair, if I had to pray for you
I can't wish anything, and I hope you knew

I can't say that I'm not fine even if I could
Can't pretend to be alright, if I should,
In the river of misery, where I could use a friend
I can't say I'm not fine, losing the pretend

And then I can't make you feel for me,
Under the weather of obsession and irony
In the world so variable, where nothing stays,
You can't feel for me, so I replace.

WISH YOU WERE POETRY

I wish you were poetry
If that, you'd come out like a perfect story
With a beautiful start and a happy ending,
Just an unending cassette, that feeling
I wish you were poetry

You'd slip out of skin as an ecstasy
In a world that's not too friendly,
You'd be what I hoped for you to be,
But then I wished you were poetry

Strangled in words, ending tragically,
Lost in translation, just a made up story
Trying to make sense, failing miserably,
That's how I wished you were poetry

Lost my words now, the sight isn't pretty,
I've been holding on to the same dead memory
Walking down the lane, I've seen the haunting past I used to bury,
I wish I knew back then, you weren't poetry

You were just a cruel word, a curse to my poetry,
Blotting my paper with nothing but treachery,
I wish u knew you weren't the part of my perfect story,
Too good to be true, I knew you weren't poetry

NEVER UNKNOWN

And if I won't make it one day
If my dreams aren't here to stay
I'd want you to know that I'll still be there
With my words, looking everywhere
For a little pinch of hope hiding away
Because I know that for every dark night, there's a bright day

If my words aren't enough for me anyway
If there is just nothing left to say
I'd want you to know that I'll still be there
With nothing but still happy, which would be rare,
For a gleam of dust and a hint of rain,
Because I know that there's true happiness after longing pain

And if I don't stay longer than I said I would,
If I live my life thinking I wish I could,
I'd want you to know that my words would still be there
Giving hope to the ones with hurt and despair,
For a little bit of kindness and love ever shown,
To be the one lost but never unknown

REALITY

Don't say no, I'm not that strong,
Trying to pretend, it's all a broken farce
I'm not that someone that never breaks,
Never was, is or will be so brave
Forgive me if I look too deep,
Into your soul, taking a leap,
From these insecurities and darkness of my mind,
To a broken memory stuck on a rewind
Don't ask me why I look so done,
I've been around and I trust no one,
The mask is up, the walls are built
Staying in here now, the bricks of guilt,
These lanes I own are cold all night,
No one's here and it feels alright
These bridges seem empty but they don't ever break,
Newer than ever, pretending, but just so fake
The truth is that I can't afford to buy a reality
I can't afford to buy a reality and isn't it so true
Everything real and true has always affected you

THE STORYTELLER

I'm looking at you, standing here
If you only knew my thoughts, insincere
The tragedy is that I never knew
Cannot trust anyone the way I do
Letting go of secrets might take you to your hearse
This is real life, I said, no time to rehearse
And then your little stories, painting me
A muse for your plain angst and insecurity
Covered in white lies and nothing true
Play your cards right, people may not always believe you
Trouble finding plot twists, who knew what I chose instead
Maybe you're a savior or maybe you're just dead
Those parts of me being the victim, I hope they aren't true
I don't like being someone, someone like you
I'd either play the devil than distressed damsel so naive
Maybe I will see you again, my stories in your grave

COUNT ON YOU

And if I told you that I didn't really know
That broken petals do not grow
Those lonely eyes shall never see
Would you put down your walls, believe me?

If I told you that I was naive
To the hazard, pretending brave
Numb with thoughts, solemn so,
Would you cross the bridge and let me know?

And if my mind feels nothing at all, again
If there's no sunshine in my life after rain
If I can't smell the petrichor, feel the way
I was supposed to, would you calm my nerves down and just stay?

If those thoughts of mine, betray again,
And all I ever feel is numbing pain,
The walls shall build up, the bridges shall break,
Would you come again, putting everything at stake?

But if I never knew anything, I'm sure that I shall know,
Those autumn winds and glistening snow,
The way I held the door and how I knew
If I wasn't me, I could count on you

THE CLASSIC

Empty rooms and open graves
That's what happens when nothing stays
The scent will be forgotten, the hues will lose
The very colors of yours that shall make the truce
Those lonely pages shall sing your praise
The dusted books, set ablaze
Your memories shall evolve the same story
You live life and then there's just a boring old tale for everybody
That monotonous drum, everyone loathes in today
However what's new with your beat, they'll say
The world goes on, and then there's no tale to pretend
Of you trying to get a true stability, a friend;
A perfect story, family and a workplace
Tales of your young teenage and childhood days
But then again, isn't everything so true
To everyone as you
As everyone living your story again
Ending up in same places and lanes
And withering away in the sorrow of dismay
Wishing you lived longer and your dreams, they stay
Wishing you didn't live longer but more
Wishing you didn't regret what you did before
But that's the real myth and couldn't be more true
In the end, the most relatable classic is you

YEARS AGO

I remember years ago
The main purpose was just to know
Not learn, not prove, a myth or reality
But to believe what we used to see
The times have changed, the days are gone
The late nights are the newer dawns
Glass slippers, no more a fairytale
Belief in happy endings have grown frail

I remember that unsetting noise
People real, not filtered with grace or poise
Brushed with the truth, no white lies
Respect truly earned by the old and wise
The mornings busy, yet so pure of light
Birds around, chirping, taking a flight
A wonderful day was what we knew
Earlier, now that just seems untrue

And when we are old and foolish, indeed
A bent tree shall speak to the rotten seed
We remember how the days used to be
Once bound by the time, yet still free
The children laughing loud, that sounds silly
So silly until now when we couldn't hear any
We saw the light of the day, no saved memory
I said I remember that time fleeting so easily
Now that time is fading but so are we

SOMEONE LIKE YOU

Those petals flew with the wind and who knew
They'd never bloom again as something new
And the end is certain for every one
You might know it, you've lost someone

Fire spreads and ashes everywhere
A battlefield, nothing's fair
You live and last and then you're gone
Last day and sadder is the dawn

Those ashes travel with the wind and lost
Life gets tougher but at what cost ?
Days pass by and you're an old story
The battles you fought, lost all the glory

And one day, you wake up learning you're free
Free from all the hazards, tryst and misery
That day, you'll see buds waiting to bloom again
And know that there's rainbow after every rain

You'll see the glory of the lost time and days
How you could've seen the nature's beautiful ways
How your thoughts could have been consumed with love
Where your misery and suffering held on like a glove

You live and last, no eternity
No time for goodbyes or a lost story
You could be happier and still brand new
A story to be told and someone so true
Someone like you

DEAR DIARY

I wrote in my book, dear diary
Last week has been crazy
My words don't match my mind
And my emotions are nowhere to find
There has been days when I was left all alone
And now I stand here staring at the phone
Hoping someone calls me up to ask me how I've been
How they felt when I wasn't to be seen
Anywhere, how did they cope
With the rumors of my dying hope
Did it feel fine like any other without me
Or did they wonder how it would be
If they didn't get to see me like today
Or the past week that has been trying to get me not to stay
The world seems busy and the nights are lonely
Every minute of the day goes by slowly
Fingers trembling and now the door is open for the last time
Last entry of my diary, lost poem, last rhyme
And now the phone finally rings and it goes dead
Just like my hope, that was enough said

STONES AND PEBBLES

Where shall you go?
When there's no soul you know
In the empty open space,
When shall you find
A person who can see through your mind
And call you on the pretend
What shall you do?
When you can't even trust a few,
And there are days when doubt surrounds you
What do you think about,
Everyone finding out
Of your secrets deep inside your head
Whom shall you trust?
When deep settles the dust
In your love and lies
Where does your mind go?
When you insecurities start to show
And you're trapped inside your skin
How do you deal with
Your thoughts and chaos closely knit
With your dusted dues and trusted paths

And how do you know
When someone can't trust you so
You try everything to make it work
But then fall apart again
That is how I seemed to know
Where I could go, where I'd find a person as such
What could I do when I'd fail to touch
A person's heart made of stone
And I knew I'd rather fall apart all alone.

SANDCASTLES

There were times when my eyes were glued to the door
Waiting impatiently for someone, ship to a shore
Now the door doesn't get knocked upon anymore
You grew up and people grew sore

I Used to put my ear out for the latest of tales
How the ship stood tall and then it sails,
Now my eyes see it all, everything seems frail
Those eyes were then of colors and now stand pale

Nights were long, dreams were scary,
Used to stay up all night, another one I couldn't dare see,
And now I sleep longer and it's funny
I sleep to escape my entity and reality

Those times were when I raced to the finish line,
All I knew was that everyone was mine
Now I still race, I race through my mind,
Past all the people, I say that I'm fine

Times when my smile was genuine and true,
Life seemed fun, everything was new,
And now I dust my old pictures and then I came through
An old picture where I was with the people I really knew

So, people changed and I grew
Smiles weren't as genuine and true,
And my eyes had stopped dreaming too
Ran faster now, that's how I knew

IF THERE WAS

If there was a better place where I could go
If there were better people I could know
If I could fall asleep every day
Knowing that life would get better as they say
But does it ever, get better than this,
Will people ever get the justice
The eyes await the future as they peep through the despair
The people are filtered, their intentions bare
The tension fills the room, cut it through with a knife
Await the better future, stagnant is their life
Things change and so do people as time goes by
And intentions change like the weather, no time for goodbye
There's another story for another day, people shall remain
As long as their words mean and longer if they gain
Another future peeps through and now there's no story to say
The words more, but in shards of gray.
Disappointing, strange and unknown it remains to be
Their story does end, times do change and then nothing's left to see

PORTRAIT

And the words know and recognize, fail as they do
It hurts to say you recognize someone you once knew
The goodbyes are long and the words fall short
I don't have any regrets, nothing of that sort
You can paint a picture, channel an image of mine
I've been watching, they know that image and I'm totally fine
My paint's dried off and now I lack to paint you,
Twenty stories left and time is now an issue
The canvas empty and my fingers seem to struggle with
The image of yours, breathes and loathes in it
I scribble down to the last word, and now it's way too late
Carved out your horrible image, and it was a portrait

PEOPLE AREN'T POETRY

So diverse, alone and variable
They remain to be,
Takes a second to realize people aren't poetry
They don't sync, love or join to make sense,
Their enemies have same name as their friends
They are all in line, in search of glee
Judging is their skill, rich, poor, black and skinny
Have you ever noticed how people aren't poetry?

They sell their opinions for some fame,
Replace, change and never stay the same
They hate the words that seems so true,
Criticize you for being you
Speak between the lines, so complicated,
Choose opinions even when facts are stated
The epitome of how you shouldn't be
Don't you realize how people aren't poetry?

Raging wars, guns and battle cries,
Fire of hatred always flickers, never dies
They pick their wars on the weak,
Then pray to Lord, salvation they seek
Spread rumors is all they can do,
They will teach you how to not be you
They shall put a noose on you as you disagree
You must know now people aren't poetry,

Those walls they built aren't even theirs
So innocent, pure and cruelly mere
They shall kill your hopes and smile at you
Talk, gossip, lie to name a few
Turn your dying fires into embers
And one day you shall remember
Saying I knew what I once wanted to be
Then I realized that people weren't poetry

NAIVE

And I could leave if I wanted to
But I didn't know how to tell you that it wasn't true
All the things you heard of me
It really isn't what you thought it to be
And I'm pacing down the hall
Looking at your face
It doesn't seem so nice
It lacks luster and grace
I fell apart there and I couldn't ever know why
I break pretty things and complain when they die

THE LAST TIME

And the last time I ever saw you
You were someone that I knew
So much that I could say
All about your egotistical and selfish ways
Because the last time I saw you
You were black and I was blue
Watered it but it never grew.
The dawn never bore nor the dusk ever will
It rains and pours endlessly down the window sill,
The paper boats drown and never shall sail
Full of life then and now you're all pale
You take down the pictures and feel insane
Your portrait empty, just remains
Those eyes that looked but never came home
Stranded down deserted, with someone but alone
That's the last time I ever saw you
You keep your eyes just blank, I don't get the clue
Those waters flowed down and they always will
They shall never wait and never just hold still
That last time burned just right in my mind
I could still see you, still felt a little blind
And that's the last time I ever shall see you
You'd be someone I always never knew

I AM NOT A BEAUTIFUL POETRY

It's not okay if they tell you
How to act or how to be
I'm real here, this is me
After all I am not a beautiful poetry

I'm not neatly packed, I'm all broken
My secrets, my lies, all deep sunken
I still don't, what you want me to see
However I am not a beautiful poetry

They say be poised, sit still look nice
Wait for your turn, then roll the dice
Bat your eyes, look ahead and smile
To reach a place, walk an extra mile
When I don't do what you say I disagree
Look at me, I am not a beautiful poetry

Notice them acting nonchalant and vain
Realizing I won't be them again
You're too vague, be a little pretty
They tell you things and it's all for free
You see I am not a beautiful poetry

I'm something you never thought I'd be
Troubled mess but still carefree
Talking to you I realized me
I'm glad I am not a beautiful poetry.

STRANGERS

It's so sad that everything is starting to die
The oceans in which we sailed earlier have started to dry
Those winds which flew with our hair have gone by
It's so sad that the time has begun to fly
The long nights of endless conversations have met their deadline
And now there's no one to call mine
It's so sad that even with it I'm totally fine
The understanding between us has started to fade
The strong bridges are breaking which we made
And it's sad to see the time passing by
Those were the times when checking up wasn't called to pry
We grew up in our ways
Same thing, every day,
But those days which we had are not here
It's the end of the times I fear
I'm hoping it won't fade away so soon
The laughter and joy under the moon
It seemed so magical it's like a fantasy
But now we're sipping on ecstasy
Isn't it funny how it's not us anymore
How can we be the same when we've shaken the core
The time made us so distant that we don't believe it
That it was us which made the moonlight lit
But it was time and it began to fade
It was strangers what it made

SORE HEART

A sore heart can take no more,
Due to fresh scars and pains from before,
It has survived the worst of the days
But it still lives on hoping on a miracle

A sore heart seeks salvation
Despite the bounds of frustration
It has sailed on every sinking ship
But still want to take a holy dip

A sore heart aches a lot
Remembering all the battles it fought
It says they are not worth it
But still looks at oneself as a misfit

A sore heart falls from every height
Just for seeking a little bit of light
It does not want stardom or Fame
But it only wants to end a game

A sore heart does not weep
Even having pains buried deep
It plasters a smile on its face
But it still behind in its race

A sore heart does not complain
Even if his hard work goes in vain
It just looks upon the sky,
But never wishes to ask why

A sore heart at last cries and does
Painfully in a corner it lies
It does not wish for a knock upon the door
But it wishes for a heart no more sore

I HAVE QUESTIONS

Dear You,
Do you feel empowered today?
Or is there nothing left to say
Are you in the shadows of pretend?
Knowing everyone yet having no friend,
Or are you just happy to be the one
Without any company.

How do you do,
When the everything goes against you
And the sun scalds your hopes and dreams
Knowing, nothing is as it seems
Then tell me,
How do you do?

What do you say,
To yourself as you walk away,
From everything that you could've been,
The people you could've known, the things you could've seen
Just to know that you're going home,
Again at dusk, to be all alone

How do you lie,
When you say you're just fine,
Life's been alright again
And doctors assure clinically sane,
But then, why do you lie,
That a part of you doesn't die,
When they ask you these questions

ANONYMOUS

Just another person with a mediocre name
Living a life of subtle anonymity and shame
Peers through the doors of what it could've been
Drenched and soaked in regrets, yet so clean

EVERYTHING HAS CHANGED

Everything has changed
Don't you feel it too
Everyone's watching, eyes on you
Your life never seemed so new
Everything has changed
And now I believe it too
Stopped talking and the distance grew
Strangers now, not an issue
It was all red and now it's all blue
You feel it now don't you?
Everything has changed
So reluctantly true
Tired of games now,
Not picking up a clue
Instead of one heart you break two
Everything has changed
And then I knew
That everything that's changed is none but me
My thoughts make me caged
I stay freed
The strangers I knew
The distance I grew
Everything and everyone had changed
That I could see
I never saw it coming, it was all me.

FIRE

And I lost the battle I never fought
I never had and left me distraught
The words I read are coming true
And now I blame none but you
That hollow smile does nothing but pretend
The damaged roads left forgotten to mend
But this is life, unseemingly fair
You get what you give, your perfect share
Of denial, anger, rebuttal and lies
That tendency to strangle until something dies
To ambush a dying fire, so cold as ice,
It's just what it is, cruelty is playing nice
Scared of everything, shall the sheep live long?
Or shall it survive there just to encounter with everything wrong?
The words were true then, and so is today
Hasn't anyone warned, fire isn't meant to play?

THORNS ARE TO STAY

Those butterflies in the stomach turned to dust
And that dust now settles in my eyes
I could've told you what was on my mind
I didn't, those eyes were too trust blind

Petals withered in my book, now they're old
You believe every little thing once told
Your ears would listen still your eyes would mislead
You water your thoughts, drenched is your seed

That knife shall still catch up to you, buried so deep
It was soiled long ago, and now you reap
Your mistrust and your anger will root this way
Those flowers shall settle, thorns are to stay

Now your plant shall grow up with no seeds to bear
A new era, new issues with no one to care
The soil shall still be watered and be fed
But the thorns stay whilst the plant be dead

BUT YOU'RE TOXIC

You're the poison draining out my touch
You're the envy, playing pretend as my grudge
Don't look deeper, might drown in lies,
Might pretend to be worse than I realize

You're the hatred clinging to my breath,
You lose me stronger than I let
I said, don't leave me alone, you're the only one,
Keeps me up at night, when I don't have anyone

You're the treachery waiting at my door,
You're someone I don't want to know anymore
I prayed and asked you to stray away to those;
Dark corners of my mind, messed up pretty close

But you're the insanity that keeps me alive,
You're the despair with a backstabbing knife
I whispered slowly, that I wonder why I think,
You're still the poison I want to drink

WALK AWAY

And I said let's walk away,
Nothing here seems to stay,
The path's broken and the myth is true,
Don't want you to be someone I once knew

GOT A SECRET

And I know myriad,
Skeletons you had,
Hiding in your closet,
Treacherously giving them away,
To someone like me
Because everyone knows my name,
But nobody, my story
Pretend, callous, hollow,
Screams my story
And you think you know me,
So pretentiously true
A part of me, I'd give away,
Still be unknown to you
You tell me your what you feel,
What you heard and your misery,
You give me a part of you
But I walk away with your story
So I know a myriad,
Skeletons in your closet
You know my name,
But not more in, than I let
So, you hold your caskets and now I got the key,
The closet of your mind, the insanities of your mystery

CHAOS

And it dawns every morning to me,
How everything in this world seems to be
Silent in the mere chaos and the settled dust,
Everyone to know, no one to trust

A BEAUTIFUL DISGRACE

Tell me then,
Who's lonelier than the moon, today?
Because I've never seen such a beautiful disgrace,
Straying tonight, just to replace,
A brighter version of itself

Tell me then, I plead you,
What's lonelier than a shadow wearing the misery of;
The subtle sadness painted all across ?
Are you as lonely as the moon tonight,
Hurting again, to be that someone bright

IF I KNEW

If I knew how it was all to end,
How the flowers wither away and bend
And the fire spreads every place until
There's no place left or nothing's still

If you knew how it all goes down,
Would you then give up your crown,
Would you live in your pretty little town,
Or would you stay, merely so

If you knew you could never stay,
And be there, never a day,
Would you fall from grace, to make it work,
Or dig your grave because endings irk

This is the tale, everything ends,
Nothing stays and nature tends
To make you feel like a fresh breath of air,
That never ends but still is rare,
Just like your life, so beautifully mere

SEARCHING

And I don't seem to know you
Fall apart, the usual way,
I want to tell you so much but I say
I lost myself trying to find you,
When I found you, you were something new
And I missed me because I loved me more
I spend days sorting my old pictures on my bedroom floor
Realized that I smiled better, genuine and true
Didn't spend nights overthinking minor issues
Didn't say I was fine when I was not,
I didn't filter my voice nor my thoughts
I was me and now I miss everything
How naive was I to search for you,
I search for red in shards of blue
Pictures remain in frames, they fall down the shelf
I found everything when I found myself

WHEN YOU WERE GONE

Those heart beats raised and never calmed down again,
And the dust on those pages will still remain,
A new chapter of a new era won't be told again,
Those paper boats shall also drown drenching in the rain,
The people will forget your name and then,
Remember what happened to you and when,
That smile appears those cheeks of drought,
And those lips dried and worn out
I wish I could tell you how it all was true,
It didn't rain when you were all alone,
But it rained when you were gone

THE WRONG ANSWERS

And that's the last time I let you stay
Can you see us, slipping away
Into the dark embers of flame,
But can't I wish for us to stay the same?
Pretend that it's been alright again
If I could tell you I haven't said
Those stories to anyone, been so afraid,
I didn't lie, those lies were true
Secrets kept to me and you
And that was the last time I let you be
The wrong answers to my mystery.

WITHERING AWAY

The withering flower knocks upon the door,
For its beauty to be a little more,
Wishing for youth to come back again,
To shine brightly in the scorching sun after the rain

The withered flower picks up its fallen leaves,
Puts them back and still believes,
In magic, fire and flame,
The withered flower has no one but itself to blame,
For losing everything that way,
When it could've made it all to stay

All at once, the withered flower blows away,
Into the skies and into the grays,
And finds itself lost once again,
Into the dust of crowded lanes,
Passing by, it realizes its doom,
Withered flowers hence do not bloom,
They just get blown away all alone,
With no one to bleat, no one to mourn
Now the withered flower knocks upon the door,
But wishes for a change no more

ALSO CHECK OUT

NINE LIVES. THREE STORIES. ONE BOOK.
'A book with zero negative reviews till date!'
ONCE
UPON
a
TIME
'A brutally honest saga of love, dreams and real life.'
SAURAV
CHHAWCHHARIA

#ZeroNegativeReviews

"A perfect blend of romance, fiction and thrill. The plot twists and cliffhangers will make sure you finish the book in one sitting. I just can't keep away from it. This is a book you should read if you're a reader and definitely read if you're a writer."

– Dhwani Parmar

"The way the life of Samir, Rashid and slums is depicted. And that sweet love story which death overtook even before it started: clearly signifies how your potential can be wasted unknowingly, on the other hand how someone low can emerge out! Man, I want a sequel to this!"

– Kushal Raut

"As John Green said and here I quote: *Sometimes, you read a book and it fills you with this weird evangelical zeal, and you become convinced that the shattered world will never be put together unless and until all living humans read the book!* Once Upon A Time is that book. And though I want to smite you for breaking my heart again and again, I can't help but say that I'm thankful that you wrote this and you did a pretty good job in ripping my heart out but thanks anyway!"

– Anjali Dedha

Message **@iamsauravc** on Instagram to buy signed copies!